HANGED IN SHAME, STANDING IN GLORY

LIFE LESSONS FROM THE THIEF ON THE CROSS

JEFFREY J. VALERIOTI

Hanged in Shame, Standing in Glory
Life Lessons from the Thief on the Cross
by *Jeffrey J. Valerioti*

Signalman Publishing
www.signalmanpublishing.com
email: info@signalmanpublishing.com
Kissimmee, Florida

Cover art concept and design by Nicole M. Valerioti.

ISBN: 978-1-935991-68-7 (paperback)
         978-1-935991-69-4 (ebook)

Library of Congress Control Number: 2012940370

SIGNALMAN
PUBLISHING

Visit www.thiefonthecrosslessons.com for access to
the printable study guide companion to
Hanged in Shame, Standing in Glory.
This valuable Bible-study resource tool can be used
for personal devotions or small-group Bible studies
in either a 6-week or 12-week format.

For the students who have shared their lives and their hearts with me in the classroom over the last ten years. Thank you for asking countless questions that have ultimately drawn me ever closer to my Lord Jesus.

For my precious wife and children who have supported my ministry from the beginning.

TABLE OF CONTENTS

I

The Inspiration for Writing Thief on the Cross

During my years in the classroom as a Bible teacher, the question invariably arose each semester as to which of the many memorable figures in the Bible would I most like to be. The guesses that were tossed out by eager students anticipating my response included the obvious biblical heroes: Joseph, Moses, King David, Solomon, Elijah, Daniel, Isaiah, Paul, or one of the disciples – though never Judas Iscariot. While any one of those choices would be worthy of emulation, I never seemed to waiver or hesitate in my response to those expectant faces in the classroom as I simply stated, "Oh, without a doubt, I would most like to have been the thief on the cross who died with Jesus and accepted Him before His last breath."

The puzzled faces of students upon hearing the response were another fixture of each new semester. Why would one choose to be a thief, condemned to death, rather than a king, a disciple, a conquering hero, or a prophet of God? With so many heroes of the faith to choose from in God's Word, why choose to be an unnamed criminal who is referenced in but a few short verses? To me, there is no better choice than the thief and no better seat of honor than the one occupied by him during Christ's final hours on earth.

To be hanged in shame one moment, and then standing in glory the next, would perhaps be the greatest transformation recorded in the Bible. And to be with Christ during His most profound hour of suffering and separation would be the greatest tangible reminder that Christ died for a glorious purpose – to save the lost and dying from their sins and reconcile them to the Father through His blood on the cross. No one could better understand what Christ endured or more fully comprehend the desperate need of a savior than the thief on the cross. Imagine carrying the weight of your death sentence to the cross of public shame and disgrace, gasping for air, bleeding in agony, while people condemned you with their ridicule and insults. Then imagine the burden being lifted as you looked into the Savior's eyes as He uttered the words, "Today you will be with me in paradise." The thief on the cross tasted physical death at the very moment he was being handed eternal life from the only One who could grant such a request, from the One who took His place as the blood sacrifice required by God, from the King of Kings named Jesus Christ. Who wouldn't want to take the place of the one ushered into Paradise by the One who left Heaven to take His place on Calvary next to two criminals so that He could lay down His life for you and for me.

Scripture records many encounters with Christ by

those in need of a touch from the Savior. No other person in the Bible encountered the Lamb of God in the way that the thief met Jesus on a hill named Golgotha. In the midst of imminent separation from the Father, God once more displayed for His Son and for us the singular purpose and plan of salvation through the request uttered by the thief on the cross. When all hope seemed lost, God again demonstrated His mercy and His grace by restoring hope to one who thought his life was over, only to find that his new life in Christ was just beginning.

Of the many lessons gleaned from the brief account of the thief on the cross, the event that forever changed the world, occurring in the last hours of his earthly life, reveals perhaps the most important lesson learned from the life of the thief – that it's never too late for redemption. It's never too late to make the choice of accepting the free gift of eternal life, paid for by Christ Himself. It's never too late to choose Christ; no matter what sins you bring to the cross, no matter how far you've drifted from Him, or how hard you've pushed Him away, the *Savior is Waiting*, so *Come Just as You Are*.

It's Never Too Late

> Chorus: It's never too late
> It's never too late
> While my flesh feels the sting
> From each stripe on my back,
> It's never too late to call you my King.
>
> While I relive my life
> As I hang here to die

You look over at me
And wipe each tear from my eye.

With each choice that I made
As I stumbled and fell
You have taken my sins on your back
You have saved me from hell.

Chorus

It's never too late
And at your dying last breath,
You promised me Paradise,
In exchange for your death.

Chorus

While the most important lesson learned may be that it's never too late to choose Christ, there are numerous life lessons to be unlocked from this brief account of the thief on the cross. As we journey together back to the hill at Calvary, fix your eyes and your heart upon the brief exchange between two dying men – one serving a sentence as the just punishment for his own sins and the One serving the sentence for the rest of mankind. In just five verses from Luke's Gospel capturing the words spoken between the two near the hour of their deaths, God reveals to us 12 life-changing lessons that will strengthen the hearts of believers and open the eyes of the unbelievers. "The Savior is waiting; why don't you let Him come in."

II

Setting the Scene for the Three Crosses of Calvary

God unfolded His plan of salvation from the moment Adam and Eve broke fellowship with the Father in the Garden when they chose to believe the lies of Satan in satisfying the desires of their prideful hearts. That plan to reconcile His children to Himself culminated in the death of God's own Son on Calvary. The lessons illustrated in the exchange between Christ and the thief dramatically portray the humble attitude and broken human spirit with which we are all to approach the Savior in asking for His forgiveness and remembrance. This life-saving exchange of words between two men nailed to trees was nothing short of an act of worship by the penitent thief. Such an act of worship was the direct expression of the mustard seed of faith planted in the heart of the penitent thief by the One to whom the worship was directed. Those final moments in the life of the thief were devoted to the worship of the King – moments that would prepare him for an eternity of glorious worship of the Lamb in Paradise.

Woven throughout the glorious tapestry of God's

Holy Word, from Genesis to Revelation, is the Father's divine plan and purpose for relationship and fellowship known as worship. The triune God of the universe had already enjoyed perfect fellowship with the Spirit and Son before choosing the precise moment to implement His sovereign plan and purpose to magnify the worship of Him by creating man. In Genesis, God unfolded each thread of His worship tapestry, revealing a portrait of creation that culminated with His crowning masterpiece made in His own image. Designed to have an abiding relationship of love with the Father, man and woman were formed from His Word, shaped by His Hand, and placed directly in His presence in Paradise for the eternal purpose of worshipping the Creator forever. That was the shimmering portrait of worship captured in the center of God's tapestry.

The plan of worship, originated in Heaven and implemented in Eden, had an enemy who was also formed by the Hand of God, as a magnificent angel, to glorify Him on the throne of Heaven. Lucifer had a vastly different plan within his heart. His sole purpose was to erase God from the center of this worship tapestry and rob Him of His glory, by replacing the Father with a hideous portrait of pride. Satan deemed within his own dark heart that he should be the supreme object of men's worship, thereby implementing a doomed battle plan to replace God. Using deception and lies as his primary weapons of choice, Satan pursued and ensnared those who had been uniquely created by Him for worship. Disguised as a serpent, He drew the front line of battle directly through the heart of Paradise. The Deceiver entered Eden and stole the hearts of Adam and Eve who chose to believe the lies of the Enemy and rebel against their Maker, thereby breaking fellowship with the Father. By allowing sin and death to enter the scene of God's worship tapestry, Adam and Eve introduced the scarlet thread of blood into God's masterpiece.

God's chosen vessels of worship, who were to be His instruments of praise to magnify His Name, were now separated from Him by the sin of their own disobedience and rejection of the One who created them. The sixty-six books of God's Holy Word unfold the redemptive plan of God to reclaim the hearts of men and restore the broken fellowship by washing the worship tapestry clean in the atoning blood of the Perfect Lamb of God who would forever reconcile men to the Father – His own Son Jesus Christ.

As the crimson thread of worship was woven throughout the Old Testament remnant of God's tapestry, the plan of redemption was spun by the patriarchs, priests, judges, kings and prophets on a blood-soaked loom of sacrifices. The sacrificial system of worship and atonement for sin was established by God in the Law given to Moses and was implemented by Levitical priests. These chosen representatives of men before God oversaw the temple worship practices, serving as mediators between sinful men and God by offering up the prayers and sacrifices of the disobedient nation of Israel to the Great I Am. Through this temporary system of sacrifices, obedience to the Law was credited to men as righteousness, but the plan of authentic and holy worship initiated in Eden

would require a permanent and perfect sacrifice that
would cover the sin of men forever. God employed
His prophets to paint a prophetic portrait of the completed tapestry for His chosen people by pointing
them to the One who would one day hang next to
the thief on a cross as the sacrifice for our sins – the
Messiah.

The God of the Ages, whose presence dwelt with
the people first through the Tabernacle and then the
Temple, would forever change worship by robing
Himself in human flesh. In God's perfect and pre-
ordained timing, Jesus Christ, the Son of God, would
become the Living Temple of God to be sacrificed on
a cross between two common thieves for the sins of
all men, spilling his atoning blood as the full and final
payment for their rebellion and disobedience. Christ
defeated Satan forever and completed the tapestry of
worship for all who call on His Name for the forgiveness of sin. The penitent thief called upon Him with
his dying breaths, asking to be remembered by Christ
when He came into His kingdom. The Apostle Paul
pointed to this moment chosen by the Father in his
letter to the church at Galatia:

> But when the time had fully come, God sent
> his Son, born of a woman, born under law, to
> redeem those under law, that we might receive
> the full rights of sons. (Galatians 4:4-5, *NIV*)

Physical buildings overseen by chosen priests
were eternally replaced by the High Priest Jesus
who, in order to complete the Father's glorious worship tapestry, tore the fabric of the Temple Veil in

two by His death on the cross and reconciled God
and men for all eternity through His Resurrection
and Ascension to the Right Hand of God. Fulfilling
His promise to those who would carry on His work
until His return in glory, Jesus sent the Holy Spirit
to live in the hearts of those who accepted His gift,
thereby building His bride – the living stones of the
church – into a spiritual house declaring the praises
of God. The final golden thread of the tapestry will
be sewn by the Hand of the Father only when He
sends His Son to gather the church and again make
His dwelling with men in the New Jerusalem. There
we shall remain with Him and worship Him forever
alongside the thief who had but one request before
he took his last breath on earth – to be remembered
by the King. The return to Paradise fulfilled by the
Lamb of God.

> As you come to him, the living Stone—reject-
> ed by men but chosen by God and precious to
> him— [5]you also, like living stones, are being
> built into a spiritual house to be a holy priest-
> hood, offering spiritual sacrifices acceptable
> to God through Jesus Christ…But you are a
> chosen people, a royal priesthood, a holy na-
> tion, a people belonging to God, that you may
> declare the praises of him who called you out
> of darkness into his wonderful light. (1 Peter
> 2:4-5, 9; *NIV*)

III

Summary of the Passages in
Mark and Luke:
What We Know/What We Don't Know

Most people associate the images at Calvary with the depiction of three crosses on a hill. This portrait is painted in hymns, poetry, artwork, and literature. For believers, it has become mere common knowledge from the historical perspective that Christ died alongside two criminals that day outside the walls of Jerusalem. The re-telling of the story in Sunday school classes traditionally includes the illustration of three crosses depicting Christ in the foreground with two men set back on either side. Christians believe, however, not as a matter of historical perspective or lessons recalled from Sunday school as a child, but because God's Word records the event as a fulfillment of prophecy and documents the words spoken from the cross that day on Calvary.

But what do we really know of the men who died alongside Christ that day on Golgotha? How old were they, and what crime could they have committed to earn a death sentence? Were they accomplices of the murderer Barabbas, the man chosen over Jesus to be set free? Did they have families with children of their own? What were their lives like? Why was Jesus placed in the middle of these two known criminals to share in the final condemnation known as the curse of crucifixion?

While God's Word offers few details in answer to the questions, theologians, scholars, philosophers and writers have speculated rather liberally, and sometimes rather creatively, on the subject in the hopes of supplying the missing pieces to the lives of the thieves. Professor William Barclay shares a number of the more imaginative literary attempts in his commentary on the Gospel of Luke, but not before providing sound biblical footing as it relates to the last question above. "It was of set and deliberate purpose that the authorities crucified Jesus between two known criminals. It was deliberately so staged to humiliate Jesus in front of the crowd and to rank him with robbers."[1]

Curiosity about these two men, who were part of the most significant event in human history, has prompted writers to fill in the details for us. Historical fiction has been penned, vividly inventing a compelling story of lives lost in hopelessness and the sins of the world, only to be redeemed for one man at the last possible moment by the Master Himself.

> Legend has been busy with the penitent
> thief. He is called variously Dismas, De-
> mas, and Dumachas. One legend makes
> him a Judaean Robin Hood who robbed

---

1   William Barclay, *The Gospel of Luke* (Louisville: Westminster John Knox Press, 2001), 339.

the rich to give to the poor. The loveli-
est legend tells how the holy family were
attacked by robbers when they fled with
the child Jesus from Bethlehem to Egypt.
Jesus was saved by the son of the cap-
tain of the robber band. The baby was so
lovely that the young brigand could not
bear to lay hands on him but set him free,
saying, 'O most blessed of children, if
ever there come a time for having mercy
on me, then remember me and forget not
this hour.' That robber youth who had
saved Jesus as a baby met him again on
Calvary; and this time Jesus saved him.[2]

While legend might paint a compelling story that
satisfies the curiosity of those who hunger for details,
Scripture tells us nothing of the men other than what
is recorded in the Gospels of Luke and Mark. Seven
verses reveal to us all that we know from the Word of
God. Those seven verses do not provide the specific
details to fill in the blanks of these men's stories, but
they tell a much larger story that has altered countless lives over the last 2000 years.

Without drawing from historical fiction, let's take
a moment to examine the verses directly from God's
Word that tells the story of these condemned criminals who shared the hill where Jesus surrendered
His life. Mark's brief account, consistent with the
journalistic pace of his entire gospel, consists of two
verses found in Chapter 15:

2   Ibid., 339, 340.

> [27]And with him they crucify two thieves;
> the one on his right hand, and the other on
> his left. [28]And the scripture was fulfilled,
> which saith, "And he was numbered with
> the transgressors."

Based solely on the words given to Mark regarding the account, we learn that the two men were transgressors, specifically thieves, who were crucified for their crimes. We also learn the physical proximity of each of their crosses in relation to Christ's. Perhaps most significant of all, Mark tells us that these two men were part of God's fulfillment of Scripture predicting that the Christ would be counted amongst the sinners as a criminal. That's it. Unless we embellish the story with fictional supporting details, we learn nothing of the paths these two men traveled leading to Calvary. We do know however that God had a specific plan and purpose for their lives in fulfilling prophecy.

The physician and gospel writer Luke provides far more detail in his narrative, something that one would expect from the exacting nature of a doctor striving to document the account for historical accuracy. In the telling of the events from Luke's gentile perspective, we receive the keys to unlock the twelve life lessons given to us from the heart of God. Five brief but powerful verses are recorded in Dr. Luke's account that includes the dialogue between Christ and the thief who made the choice in death to accept the gift of eternal life – the subject of our first lesson: the choice is life or death.

> [39] One of the criminals who were hanged there was hurling abuse at Him, saying, "Are You not the Christ? Save Yourself and us!"
>
> [40] But the other answered, and rebuking him said, "Do you not even fear God, since you are under the same sentence of condemnation?
>
> [41] "And we indeed are suffering justly, for we are receiving what we deserve for our deeds; but this man has done nothing wrong."
>
> [42] And he was saying, "Jesus, remember me when You come in Your kingdom!"
>
> [43] And He said to him, "Truly I say to you, today you shall be with Me in Paradise." (Luke 23:39-43, NASB)

Luke's expanded account sheds considerably more light on the characters and words of the two thieves than Mark's brief summary of the same event. Much of what we learn about the criminals unfolds in the last words of the penitent thief as he first rebukes the unrepentant thief and then turns to Jesus with the final request of his earthly existence.

As to the lives of the men, Luke's verses reveal little more than Mark's two verses about the actual identities of the two thieves. While we are not able to trace their individual paths leading to Calvary, Luke's readers are left with little doubt as to the eternal destinations of the men beyond Calvary. The first

life-lesson from the two thieves was played out on
Calvary. Based upon the words uttered by each man,
we are made witnesses to one man's rejection and
ridicule of Christ and to the other's acknowledgment
of Jesus as King. One man chose to follow the world
and hurled abuses, while the other expressed fear of
God and fixed his eyes on Christ. One man ordered
Jesus to save them, the other asked simply to be remembered. One man proclaimed their guilt, and that
same man declared Jesus' innocence. That thief entered paradise, while the other entered hell. One man
accepted eternal life, the other chose death. It was a
choice. Lesson #1: The choice is life or death.

Before exploring the life-lessons revealed to us
through Luke's account of the two thieves, we must
first undertake a thorough word study of the verses.
A deeper understanding of God's message can then
be reinforced upon our hearts as we apply the lessons to our daily lives. Proper exegesis of the passage includes examination of the key Greek words
originally scribed by Luke, as well as the context of
the chosen words, in order to arrive at an accurate
interpretation of the account's meaning. So, we turn
our focus and attention upon a study of the five verses that vividly capture and contrast the choices made
by the two thieves in their final hours on earth.

IV

Exegesis of the Luke Passage and Commentaries Analysis

The account of the two thieves in Luke 23 paints the most vivid imagery in Scripture of conversion in the plan of salvation. God portrays the stark contrast of two men at completely opposite ends of the salvation spectrum – one man angrily rejecting Christ and seeking to cling to his earthly life and the other man acknowledging the deity of Jesus and seeking favor in the life to come. In order to properly apply the meaning of the verses to our daily lives in the here-and-now, we must first grasp the intended meaning in the there-and-then. More succinctly stated in theological terms, we must engage in the exegesis of the passage before we move on to the hermeneutics.

While a thorough study of the account from the perspective of systematic theology is beyond the scope of this book, a brief survey of scholarly journals and commentaries on the Luke passage invariably centers upon a common thread in the tapestry of the story. Most theological analyses focus upon the intended meaning of Jesus' words concerning the timing and the place of which Jesus spoke in His response to the penitent thief's request to remember him. Academic discussions and religious debates inevitably distill the source of disagreement down to the proper interpretation and implications of two words: *today* and *paradise*. Most evangelicals point to the Luke 23 passage as foundational support for the argument that believers in Christ are immediately present in spirit with the Lord in heaven upon their physical deaths on earth. Others contend that etymological errors in translating the original Greek have resulted in misinterpretations of the statement made by Christ. A minority of Christian groups, scholars, and academicians advocate a theory of "soul sleep" and assert that the response from Jesus pointed to the future and His coming Kingdom during the Millennial Reign.

Resolution of the issue requires a deeper understanding of the words themselves and a thorough analysis of both sides of the relevant theological issues and supporting doctrines. Again, such analysis is beyond the scope of this book, as there are volumes of books and articles devoted to the subject. However, a brief survey of key linguistic points sheds considerable light on the interpretation of the passage and will perhaps spark further, more intensive study on the related topics.

With regard to the immediacy of Jesus' ushering the repentant criminal into paradise, the question of "soul sleep" arises as a plausible explanation for the statement made to the thief in connection with the word "today." Essentially, the doctrine of "soul sleep" holds that upon death the soul "sleeps" and is not conscious until the resurrection of the body. While there are a number of times in Scripture when "sleep" is used as a euphemism for death (Luke 8:52; John 11:11; Acts 7:60; 1 Corinthians 15:18, 20, 51; 1 Thessalonians 4:14-15; 5:10), there are other passages making it abundantly clear that the soul is NOT unconscious until the resurrection (2 Cor. 5:8 and Phil. 1:23). Additionally, in two passages of 1 Peter, Jesus "preached to the spirits in prison" after His crucifixion and before His resurrection (1 Peter 3:19; 4:6). Regardless of the definitive interpretation of these and other passages, the verses do not contradict Jesus Christ inw the Spirit from ushering the penitent thief into paradise.[3] But what was the intended timing of the promise being fulfilled?

Different interpretations of the verses even arise as a result of misplacement of the seemingly insignificant comma in writing. Examination of early Greek manuscripts of the New Testament reveals there was no punctuation in them. Editors added punctuation at a later date to facilitate reading of the text. Punctuation subsequently became a matter of editorial interpretation and therefore did not always reflect the originally intended meaning of the author, depending upon the placement of the punctuation marks. What if the comma that is traditionally placed before the word "today" in many translations of Luke 23:43 were placed after the word?

Scholars have recognized that "today" is often used as a Hebrew way of stressing a command

---

3   Dr. Ralph F. Wilson, Disciple Lessons from Luke's Gospel, (http://www.jesuswalk.com/lessons/23_39-43.htm).

or promise. We see this repeatedly in the Book of Deuteronomy, as Moses warns the people of Israel 'today" that they must obey their God. The warning is not that they must obey Him today only, but the warning is given "today" (Deut. 4:40; 5:1; 6:6; 7:11; 8:1,11). We employ a similar emphasis in the English language when we say, "I'm telling you this right now!" Such a statement implies more than is expressed by the present tense of the verb: it means that we want the hearer to take heed to our words!

In terms of comma placement within Luke 23:43, a re-reading of the verse with a repositioned comma after "today" yields the following: "Truly I tell you today, you will be with me in paradise." (A word-for-word translation of the Greek text is: "Truly to you I say today with me you will be in the paradise.") With such a rendering, the emphasis is on the promise itself – that of being with Jesus in paradise. The word "today" is there to give solemn and emphatic assurance that the promise will indeed be fulfilled. In the final analysis, does the shifting of a comma alter the meaning or change the intent of what Jesus promised the thief in their final exchange on earth? The fact remains that Christ assured the repentant, dying man on the cross beside Him that he would indeed be in "paradise" with Christ. Placing the comma before or after "today" does not alter where the thief will be spending eternity. He **will** be with Jesus in paradise.

The author of the Gospel was not present at the crucifixion to hear Christ's comment personally. Christ's comment was recorded from the *oral* tradition of the disciples. This leads us to the second point: that the oral tradition had preserved this comment in a particular form, with the *spoken* emphasis already built into it. Commas have no syntactical value in New Testament Greek. If commas are later introduced by an editor, they would serve only to make the text easier to read — not to clarify the meaning. Commas, in any edition of the Greek New Testament, are intended only as a help to the reader, not as a means of safeguarding the correct understanding of a passage. In view of the above details, the presupposition that the text of Luke 23:43 is ambiguous without the comma is not legitimate.[4]

This turns the discussion of proper interpretation toward the meaning of the word "paradise" in the Luke account. The fact that the Greek text reads "the" paradise suggests that "Jesus has in mind the definite and well-known paradise described in Scripture – the Garden of Eden restored. 'Paradise' is not simply a vague concept, denoting a condition of bliss, as it has come to be used. It is a specific place that will be restored at a specific time!"[5]

4   The Comma of Luke 23:43, Grace Communion International, 1989, http://www.wcg.org/lit/prophecy/comma.htm
5   William M. Wachtel, A Study of Luke 23:43, http://www.scribd.com/doc/7002467/A-STUDY-of-LUKE-2343-by-Pastor-William-M-Wachtel

Our English word "paradise" is a transliteration of
the Greek word *paradeisos*, the word used for *paradise* in the Septuagint, the Greek translation of the
Old Testament. The Greek term is actually Persian
in origin and translates as "park" or "garden." Referring to the Garden of Eden in Genesis 2 and 3,
the word is again used in Revelation to refer to the
restored paradise over which Jesus will reign on the
New Earth after His Second Coming.[6] Judaism of Jesus' day equated Paradise with the New Jerusalem,
and saw it as the present abode of the souls of the
departed patriarchs, the elect, and the righteous. In
the New Testament the word paradise is used three
times:

"Today you will be with me in **paradise**." (Luke
23:43)

"And I know that this man -- whether in the body
or apart from the body I do not know, but God knows
-- was caught up to **paradise**. He heard inexpressible
things, things that man is not permitted to tell." (2
Corinthians 12:3-4)

"He who has an ear, let him hear what the Spirit
says to the churches. To him who overcomes, I will
give the right to eat from the tree of life, which is in
the **paradise** of God." (Revelation 2:7)

In 2 Corinthians 12:3-4 Paul seems to equate the
"third heaven" with paradise, leading many religious
scholars to identify paradise with heaven. Such an
interpretation of the word leads to the conclusion that

---

6   ibid.

Jesus is indeed promising the repentant thief that he will be with Jesus in heaven.[7]

Theologians and scholars have long theorized and speculated as to the nature and physical character-istics of Heaven. While none argue that Heaven is indeed the abode of God, many dispute the attributes of Paul's "third heaven" and the timing and manner of arrival of its inhabitants. Rather than the image of a static creation serving as the dwelling place of God Almighty, Heaven unfolds throughout Scripture as an organic masterpiece being continually trans-formed by the Hand of God through the ages as the ultimate dwelling place of His Kingdom's heirs, that once encompassed "Abraham's bosom" as one of two compartments comprising *Sheol* as referenced in Jesus' parable of Luke 16.

Perhaps nowhere else in Scripture does one gain a better glimpse of the transformational shaping of Heaven by Christ than in John 14 when the Lord re-veals to His disciples where He is going. Jesus tells them that He is leaving to literally prepare an eter-nal dwelling for those that have believed in Him and called upon His Name. "We do not know the pre-cise nature of this activity, but it is apparent that He is readying a place where believers will fellowship with Him: 'In my Father's House are many rooms; if it were not so, I would have told you. I am going there to prepare a place for you. And if I go and pre-pare a place for you for you, I will come back and take you to be with me that you also may be where I

---

7   Dr. Ralph F. Wilson, Disciple Lessons from Luke's Gospel, (http://www.jesuswalk.com/lessons/23_39-43.htm).

am.' (John 14:2-3)"[8]

Based on the building metaphor that Christ Himself provided His disciples, there would not be a large leap of logic required in constructing a doctrine of Heaven that includes compartments and rooms defining the physical space of Heaven across Scripture. "Our home is being built for us by the Carpenter from Nazareth. Building is His trade... Jesus didn't say to His disciples, 'I've already prepared a place for you in heaven,' but, 'I am going there to prepare a place for you.' This means Heaven has undergone some remodeling between the time He spoke and the time we join Him there." [9]

In the Bible, there are at least five distinct phases of Heaven. There was the original Heaven prior to the entrance of sin. The next stage of Heaven was the Old Testament Heaven of "Abraham's bosom," considered by some theologians to be one of the two compartments of *Sheol.* Following the resurrection of Jesus Christ, Paradise becomes the present form of Heaven, having been relocated by Jesus from *Hades.* This is where believers now come directly into the presence of the Lord upon physical death. A fourth phase of Heaven, the millennial kingdom, is where Christ will rule over the earth with the redeemed (Revelation 20:7-10), as poetically foretold by Isaiah in Chapter 65 of his prophetic writings. Finally, the Heaven to come appears after the final judgment – the New Jerusalem in the new heavens

---

8   Millard J. Erickson, *Christian Theology* (Grand Rapids: Baker Books, 1998), 1234.
9   Randy Alcorn, *In Light of Eternity* (Colorado Springs, WaterBrook Press, 1999), 36.

and new earth (Revelation 21-22), where at last everyone will be in their glorified bodies, eternally free from sin and death. "Heaven has and will continue to undergo some changes, additions, expansions, and renovations while maintaining its core distinctive... Heaven, as it is, is not yet all it will ultimately become...Heaven past, Heaven present, and Heaven future should all be understood as Heaven, but must not be viewed as being exactly the same."[10]

If we view Christ's reply through the lens of a two-compartment theory of Heaven, we would interpret the words spoken by Jesus to the penitent thief as the emphatic promise of immediate residence in the phase of Heaven referred to as Abraham's Bosom. Christ's promise of paradise did not imply the thief's taking immediate residence in one of the completed "rooms of heaven" if we recall Christ's words to His disciples in John 14 about His going to prepare a place. The thief could not possibly take occupancy of a place not yet prepared by Christ Himself. This does not negate the promise of paradise, nor the immediacy of the thief's residence in heaven, especially if we view the "paradise" of which Jesus spoke as one of the phases of Heaven identified in Scripture.

Dr. Harold Wilmington of Liberty Baptist Theological Seminary offers a poignant observation in his commentary on Luke's account of the penitent thief. As Dr. Wilmington traces Christ's "Seventy-two Steps from Glory to Glory," he notes several facts concerning salvation that are particularly evident in

10   Dave Earley, *The 21 Most Amazing Truths About Heaven* (Uhrichsville, Ohio: Barbour Publishing, Inc. 2006), 59.

the passage: 1) That salvation is offered to anyone, anywhere; 2) That salvation is by grace through faith alone, thereby refuting the doctrines of sacramentalism, baptismal regeneration, purgatory, and universalism since only one of the thieves was saved; and 3) That salvation will be rejected by some in spite of everything God can do.[11]

Here we see three men: One was dying *for* sin (the Savior). One was dying *from* sin (the repentant thief). One was dying *in* sin (the lost thief). All classes of humanity were represented at the cross. There were the indifferent, the religious, the materialistic, and the earnest seeker. The cross is indeed the judgment of this world.[12]

---

11   Dr. Harold L.Wilmington, *Wilmington's Guide to the Bible* (Carol Stream, IL: Tyndale House Publishers, Inc., 1984), 333.
12   ibid.

V

When I Survey the Wondrous Cross –
Surveying the Lessons Learned from
the Thief

Perhaps the most apparent lesson learned from the penitent thief's plea to Christ is that it's never too late to choose Christ. Yet in those five short verses from Luke's Gospel capturing the words spoken between the two near the hour of their deaths, God reveals to us 12 life-changing lessons that will strengthen the hearts of believers and open the eyes of the unbelievers. As we journey together back to the hill at Calvary, fix your eyes and your heart upon the brief exchange between two dying men – one serving his sentence as the just punishment for his own sins and the One serving the sentence for the rest of mankind. The life lessons imparted at the cross continue to transform the lives of those who make that same choice as the thief – to cry out to Jesus in faith and give up their lives to Him.

Lesson #1

The Choice is Life or Death

The choices made at Calvary carried consequences that were as diametrically opposed as could ever possibly exist in creation: life or death. Two men traveled the same road in life that ultimately led to judicial condemnation and physical death by crucifixion – the cruelest form of Roman judgment, specifically designed to inflict the greatest possible suffering, agony, and public humiliation and disgrace. Same road, same consequence, same form of capital punishment. Yet, each man was faced with one final choice before leaving his earthly dwelling.

At the disgraceful conclusion to their lives, each thief was confronted with one final decision to make. The man hanging on the cross to the right of Christ and the one on the left of Jesus each had one final choice to consider, one which carried with it the divine power to blot out his transgressions and offer a full and complete pardon of all his sins. Even more miraculous, one choice would bestow eternal life in paradise, the other an eternity in hell, the second death from which there would be no escape. As cliché as it might be to phrase the choice in this manner, it was literally a choice between life and death.

One man ultimately chose to continue following the world by joining in with ridicule and hurling insults at Christ, expending his final breaths to mockingly ask Christ to save himself. He chose death. The other thief made the choice to rebuke his accomplice while at the same time expressing fear of God and acknowledging the royal status of His Son as King. He chose life. Jesus responded by granting him entrance into paradise. The penitent thief made the choice to turn his back on the world and surrender his life to Christ by faith, trusting that he was indeed speaking to the King of Kings who would one day reign over His Eternal Kingdom. By so doing, he received the reward of eternity in Heaven with Jesus.

For all those facing the same choice, two thousand years after the clearest depiction of the conversion crossroads at Calvary, the outcomes remain unchanged and the consequences remain eternal. At the crosses of three men sentenced to die on Golgotha, God presented the world with the starkest contrast of the life-or-death choice that is required to receive the free gift of salvation. One man chose to reject the gift, while the other chose to receive the gift. The choice remains the same. Either reject Christ or accept Christ. Either endure hell or taste paradise. There can be no oversimplification of what occurred at the cross as it relates to the choices faced by these two anonymous men of history, or as it relates to their responses toward Christ. God wanted to be certain that we had a clear picture of the two roads traveled by these men as a point of reference for our own choices, our own paths, and ultimately our eternal destinations.

Life-or-death choices are apparent throughout God's Word. Adam and Eve had the same two choices presented in the Garden of Eden that were presented to the two men on the crosses next to Jesus on Golgotha. One choice would lead to continued fellowship with God, directly in His presence for all eternity: life. The other choice would lead to rejection by God as a result of disobedience, bringing sin into the perfect world God had created: death. They chose to believe the lies of Satan, ultimately choosing death over life. "For the wages of sin is death." (Romans 6:23a).

Joseph, the typology of Jesus in Genesis, similarly faced condemnation in prison accompanied by two men. Two other servants of Pharaoh, the cupbearer and the baker, found themselves thrown into prison along with Joseph. Each man spoke to Joseph about their dreams, which Joseph then interpreted for them. Foreshadowing the consequences faced by the two thieves alongside Jesus, the result of the two prisoners' dreams meant death for one of the men, and release and exaltation for the other. The Genesis 40 account of these two men with Joseph offered a glimpse of the outcomes experienced by the two criminals with Jesus: one prisoner with Jesus would die eternally, but one would taste the Living Water of Christ's promise of eternal life in Heaven.

Throughout Jesus' earthly ministry, people who followed the news of Jesus' miracles or who even had direct encounters with the Master Himself were faced with two simple and clear choices: to believe in Christ by faith or to reject by sight. As with the thieves alongside Christ or the prisoners sharing a cell with Joseph, the consequences of the choices made were the same: life or death. Perhaps the most striking example in the gospels of one who was directly confronted with this choice by Christ Himself was the story of the rich, young ruler in the Mark 10 and Luke 18 passages.

The young man specifically asked Christ what he must do to inherit eternal life. Jesus presented him with a choice to make in order to be saved: sell everything and follow Christ. Mark's account states that the man went away sad. This wealthy young man was confronted with a choice to either reject Christ's instructions, and retain his earthly wealth, or to follow Christ and exchange his worldly treasure for heavenly riches. The fact that Mark recorded the man's response as one of sadness indicates that the young ruler was unable to leave hold of his material possessions in exchange for the promise of eternal life. He literally turned his back on Jesus and went away. Just as with the angry thief on the cross rejecting Christ, this man at the other end of the socio-economic spectrum had the same choices that were presented by Christ to others: choose Christ and have life eternal or reject Him and face death. Again, the choices were clear and the outcomes the same: life or death. Simple.

Lesson #2

Making the Choice Cannot be Avoided

Procrastination is the arrow shot by Satan to attack those seeking to make a choice to follow Jesus Christ. Regardless of the rationalizations made to avoid the decision, the time arrives when a choice must be made to either accept Jesus or reject Jesus. It simply cannot be avoided. Even before their last breaths, the thieves could not avoid or put off any longer the choice that everyone must ultimately make in this lifetime to either become a follower of Jesus or a follower of the prince of this world.

These two men hanging beside Jesus did not have the luxury of postponing their choices until tomorrow. They had run out of tomorrows on this earth and had exhausted their days in the present life. Yet the choices they made in those final moments determined how they would forever spend their days in the life to come. That time arrives in each person's life when making the choice can no longer be avoided. Indecision no longer remains an option – you either choose to accept the free gift of paradise offered by Jesus or you choose to reject it.

To the all-knowing God of the Ages, this is no surprise. The infallible Creator knew us before He formed us in our mother's wombs and knows the precise number of our days. His Word declares this truth in the poetry of Job and Psalms:

> My frame was not hidden from you
>> when I was made in the secret place.
>> When I was woven together in the depths of
>>> the earth,
> [16] your eyes saw my unformed body.
>> All the days ordained for me
>> were written in your book
>> before one of them came to be.

> —Psalm 139:15-16, *NIV*

> Man's days are determined;
>> you have decreed the number of his months
>> and have set limits he cannot exceed.

> —Job 14:5, *NIV*

Fallible humans however believe they will always have a "tomorrow" available to them for making the decision to accept Christ's offer. An attitude of "living in the moment" defines the human mindset that often fuels the engine of procrastination. There are no time extensions to the pre-ordained calendar of our lives established by the Creator. The choice must be made within that divine timeframe established by God. Salvation decisions cannot be made in eternity's hindsight. Again, making the choice to follow Christ cannot be avoided. There are no "undecideds" in Hades or Heaven.

Lesson #3

It's Never Too Late to Make the Choice

Just as procrastination poses a stumbling block to making the decision to follow Christ, another arrow in Satan's quiver comes in the form of the lie that it's far too late in the sinner-seeker's life to be saved. The father of lies would have us believe that the lifetime heap of sins that seem to multiply exponentially the older we get make it impossible for God to ignore them and cover over them with forgiveness. Hopelessness becomes one of Satan's most effective weapons in this battle. Guilt on the part of the sinner perpetuates the lie, to the point that the lost soul concludes that he is indeed beyond hope and ultimately sinks deeper into the cesspool of sin and suffering.

Yet, impossibilities and hopelessness are not attributes of the God of the Ages. They are inconsistent with His nature. Jesus Himself declared to His disciples when the young, rich ruler turned his back on Jesus that nothing is impossible for God.

> [26]The disciples were even more amazed, and said to each other, "Who then can be saved?"
> [27]Jesus looked at them and said, "With man this is impossible, but not with God; all things are possible with God." (Mark 10:26, 27, NIV)

Most observers on the hill called Golgotha that day would surely have believed it was far too late for any of the condemned to receive a pardon for their sentence, much less their sins. They were already nailed to crosses, bleeding and near death by suffocation. Yet, this is precisely what the Lord Jesus offered the penitent thief during that brief exchange on Calvary. His faith not only delivered forgiveness in this life, but also eternity with Christ in Heaven.

The beauty of God's forgiveness lies in its forgetfulness. Scripture records the promise of God in several places regarding His divine ability to literally "blot out" our sins, our iniquities, our transgressions. In both Micah and Isaiah, the prophets write of God's power to "hurl all our iniquities into the depths of the sea" (Micah 7:19) and "to put all my sins behind your back." (Isaiah 38:17). The number, the severity, or the timing of the sins matters not to God. He forgives them all, and He forgets them all, when we come to Him with a repentant heart and ask His forgiveness with reverence and awe – just like the thief on the cross, and just like David prayed to God in Psalm 51, "Hide your face from my sins and blot out all my iniquity." (Psalm 51:9) There is no waiting period with God based upon the size of the sin, and there is no merit badge to be earned prior to receiving the gift of forgiveness from the Father. He removes our transgressions from us – our sins are gone, and it's never too late to ask Him to blot out a lifetime of sins, even if we are near our last breath. "As far as east is from the west, so far has he removed our transgressions from us." (Psalm 103:12)

For the God who knows no impossibilities, grant-ing new lives after the forgiveness of sin is precisely what His Son was sent in the world to accomplish. The sinners are given new lives in Christ, the sick are made well, and the hopeless are given new hope through the blood of Jesus. As we learn in reading John 11, Mary and Martha knew their brother La-zarus had died four days earlier, but it did not keep them from asking Jesus to restore him and bring him back to life. Jesus looked up to the Father, thanked Him, and asked Lazarus to step forth from the tomb. Was it too late? Most witnesses that day would have thought the task impossible since Jesus had arrived too late to save Lazarus. Those witnesses watched a man wearing grave clothes step forth from the tomb that day. It was not too late for Lazarus, because nothing is impossible with God.

The woman of John 8 caught in the act of adul-tery was certain that her life would soon be over, as the men stood above her frightened body with rocks raised over their heads, ready to condemn her by stoning her to death. Was it too late? Most bystanders that day would have thought she was simply earning the rightful consequence handed down from the Law of Moses. Those bystanders watched and listened as Christ drew with His finger into the sand and spoke the words of forgiveness that would lead the angry men to put down their stones and walk away from the woman who had just been given a new life by the Savior of the world, who told her to go forth and sin no more. It was not too late for her, because nothing is impossible with God.

Jairus was certain that his little girl was near death when he pleaded with Jesus to heal his daughter. Was it too late? According to the men who later told Jairus that his daughter was dead, the answer would certainly be yes. Mark 5:35 indicates that the men even implored the synagogue ruler to stop bothering the Teacher to help his now deceased daughter. Yet those same people who stood crying and wailing at Jairus' house watched that same little girl rise up and walk about as Christ instructed them to give her food. It was not too late for this little girl whose daddy demonstrated the faith of a giant in asking Jesus to heal his daughter with the touch of His Hand, because nothing is impossible with God.

If one reads the eye-witness testimonies detailing so many seemingly hopeless situations where Christ conquers sin and death, one could not imagine that anything is impossible for God. This applies to our sinful lives as well. It's never too late to reach out to Jesus and ask Him to touch our lives with His Healing Hand. We are given the Father's promise that He will forgive and forget our transgressions and give us new life in Christ, regardless of the number or magnitude of our sins. Just as Jairus believed in the impossible, we too must come to Christ in faith and ask Him to bring life from death. Just as the thief on the cross demonstrated at Calvary, we too must ask Christ to remember us and yet forget our sin. We have the Father's Word that He will indeed do both. "I, even I, am he who blots out your transgressions, for my own sake, and remembers your sins no more." (Isaiah 43:25).

Lesson #4

No Past Can Keep You from an Eternal Future

Typical human thought and logic lead many to assume a posture of self-reliance in straightening out life's messes, poor decisions, and splotchy pasts. The flawed thinking resembles an inescapably bad merry-go-round ride. "I've got to clean myself up and get myself straightened out before I come to Jesus." "No one could forgive what I've done." "I've made too many mistakes to be given another chance." "I've gone too far down this bad road that there is no turning back – it's just too late for someone with a past like me." Only Jesus can deliver us from the sin-distorted self-talk that seeks to drive us from the Savior. No matter what the past, no matter the level of corruption or depravity, no matter how low we've sunk, there is complete and total forgiveness in the arms of Jesus.

Jesus wrapped His loving arms around those who most needed an escape from hopeless pasts and even more desperate present circumstances. Could there possibly be such love and acceptance for one possessed of seven demons with a promiscuous reputation? Counted among the followers of Christ was one named Mary Magdalene. For Mary, her encounter with Jesus was nothing short of total transformation by the Savior.

> [1]After this, Jesus traveled about from one town and village to another, proclaiming the good news of the kingdom of God. The Twelve were with him, [2]and also some women who had been cured of evil spirits and diseases: Mary (called Magdalene) from whom seven demons had come out; (Luke 8:1-2, NIV)

Mary's faith in Jesus as Messiah led her all the way to Calvary, as she watched the One who had delivered her from demons die for the sins of the world. She did not flee from her Lord and Savior in that darkest hour. Mary refused to abandon the One who had lovingly wiped away her past and offered her a new life – an eternal life. Christ rewarded Mary Magdalene's faithfulness. While His disciples hid in the shadows for fear of public ridicule and judgment, Christ chose Mary as the one to whom He would first appear upon His resurrection. No past would keep Mary from her eternal future.

There could be no one more unworthy of the grace and mercy of Jesus than one whose past included religious training as a Pharisee and notoriety as a murderer of the followers of Christ. Certainly such a past seemed beyond the hope of redemption. Saul would soon discover that the cleansing of his past would require descent into total darkness before he would see the Light of Christ. Paul himself testified

in Acts 22:3-16 to his lowly standing as a pharisee
and a murderer of Christians, that there was no one
more unworthy of the grace and mercy of Jesus:

> [3]I am a Jew, born in Tarsus of Cilicia, but
> brought up in this city. Under Gamaliel I
> was thoroughly trained in the law of our
> fathers and was just as zealous for God
> as any of you are today. [4]I persecuted the
> followers of this Way to their death, ar-
> resting both men and women and throw-
> ing them into prison, [5]as also the high
> priest and all the Council can testify. I
> even obtained letters from them to their
> brothers in Damascus, and went there to
> bring these people as prisoners to Jerusa-
> lem to be punished.
>
> [6]About noon as I came near Damas-
> cus, suddenly a bright light from heaven
> flashed around me. [7]I fell to the ground
> and heard a voice say to me, "Saul! Saul!
> Why do you persecute me?"
>
> [8]"Who are you, Lord?" I asked.
>
> "I am Jesus of Nazareth, whom you are
> persecuting," he replied. [9]My compan-
> ions saw the light, but they did not under-
> stand the voice of him who was speaking
> to me.
>
> [10]"What shall I do, Lord?" I asked.
>
> "Get up," the Lord said, "and go into
> Damascus. There you will be told all
> that you have been assigned to do." [11]My

companions led me by the hand into Damascus, because the brilliance of the light had blinded me.

[12]A man named Ananias came to see me. He was a devout observer of the law and highly respected by all the Jews living there. [13]He stood beside me and said, "Brother Saul, receive your sight!" And at that very moment I was able to see him.

[14]Then he said: "The God of our fathers has chosen you to know his will and to see the Righteous One and to hear words from his mouth. [15]You will be his witness to all men of what you have seen and heard. [16]And now what are you waiting for? Get up, be baptized and wash your sins away, calling on his name."

Not only did Jesus wash away the sin and stains of Saul's murderous past as a persecutor of Christians, Christ ordained the reborn Paul as His chosen instrument to be a light to the Gentiles in sharing the gospel message. From the total darkness of Damascus to the streets of Rome itself, Paul would become the greatest missionary the world would ever see. No past would keep Paul from his eternal future.

Matthew's profession as a tax collector drew hatred from the people and would certainly seem to indicate no place in the Kingdom of God for one such as him. There was no occupation more reviled than the unscrupulous, cheating post of a tax collector for the Roman government. Levi, as he was known to his former friends and family, inspired both hatred and fear in his role and was viewed as a betrayer to his people. Could there be anyone more hopeless or undeserving of God's forgiveness? Jesus saw otherwise as he looked into the heart of Levi and called him to follow the only one who could forgive him and call this sinner to repentance in order to inherit an eternal future. No past would keep the Apostle and Gospel writer Matthew from his eternal future. Luke 5:27-31 (NIV):

> [27]After this, Jesus went out and saw a tax collector by the name of Levi sitting at his tax booth. "Follow me," Jesus said to him, [28] and Levi got up, left everything and followed him.

> [29] Then Levi held a great banquet for Jesus at his house, and a large crowd of tax collectors and others were eating with them. [30]But the Pharisees and the teachers of the law who belonged to their sect complained to his disciples, "Why do you eat and drink with tax collectors and 'sinners'?"

> [31]Jesus answered them, "It is not the healthy who need a doctor, but the sick. [32]I have not come to call the righteous, but sinners to repentance."

Where does one turn after 12 years of unsuccessful treatments for a medical condition whose outcome seems all but certain? For the woman with the issue of blood, all indications from her medical past would point toward a bleak future and a hopeless prognosis from a medical standpoint. But what about from an eternal standpoint? Could there possibly be hope for a future when the past was shrouded with numerous doctors, unsuccessful treatments, untold suffering, and drained financial resources? Certainly, all that remained was death as her foregone conclusion.

Yet her faith in Christ was mightier than any past disappointments or failures regarding a cure for her condition. The woman knew deep within her heart that all she needed to do was to get just close enough to Jesus to touch His garment, and she would be healed of her affliction. As she stretched out her arm amidst the crowds and strained her hand toward the Master, the woman knew she would soon be free of her pain and sufferings. Christ would release her from the bondage of her blood disorder. The time would soon come when His own blood would release her from all bondage, for all eternity. All it required was faith in the only One who had power over all things. No past would keep this woman of faith from her eternal future. No past will keep you from your eternal future when you place your trust in Christ.

> A large crowd followed and pressed around him. [25]And a woman was there who had been subject to bleeding for twelve years. [26]She had suffered a great deal under the care of many doctors and had spent all she had, yet instead of getting better she grew worse. [27]When she heard about Jesus, she came up behind

him in the crowd and touched his cloak, [28]because she thought, "If I just touch his clothes, I will be healed." [29]Immediately her bleeding stopped and she felt in her body that she was freed from her suffering.

[30]At once Jesus realized that power had gone out from him. He turned around in the crowd and asked, "Who touched my clothes?"

[31]"You see the people crowding against you," his disciples answered, "and yet you can ask, 'Who touched me?' "

[32]But Jesus kept looking around to see who had done it. [33]Then the woman, knowing what had happened to her, came and fell at his feet and, trembling with fear, told him the whole truth. [34]He said to her, "Daughter, your faith has healed you. Go in peace and be freed from your suffering." (Mark 5:24-34 NIV)

Therefore, there is now no condemnation
for those who are in Christ Jesus,
because through Christ Jesus
the law of the Spirit of life
set me free from the law of sin and death.

Romans 8:1-2 NIV

Lesson #5

There is a Consequence that Must be Paid for the Choice Made

*... you are under the same sentence of
condemnation.
And we indeed are suffering justly.
(Luke 23:40b – 41a)*

Each of the men on either side of Christ had a
choice to make in the final breaths of their condemned lives. As Luke recorded the events surround-
ing the crucifixion in his gospel, he unfolded a chro-
nology of the utterances from each man that contrast
the choices ultimately made by the men on either side
of Christ. The first recorded insults hurled at Christ
by the unrepentant thief followed the sneering of the
rulers in verse 35 and the mocking by the soldiers
in verse 36. Even in dying, this thief chose to continue following the crowd and mimicking the actions
of the world as he chose to join in and hurl insults
at the King of the Jews. Following the ways of the
world led this man on a path to the cross of execution
for the crimes committed in pursuit of worldly gain.
Facing imminent death nailed to a tree, clearly with
nowhere else to go, this man continued in the wrong

choices that led him to his own execution and made one final choice that sealed his eternity.

The other condemned criminal could have easily joined the other voices of mockery, ridicule, and rejection. His crimes on earth had brought upon himself the same fate as that of his co-conspirator and led him to the identical destination in life – this life. However, his choice in those final hours to ignore the chorus of heretical voices that denied Christ's position as Messiah and King ushered him toward a vastly different eternal destination. By proclaiming his fear of God along with his own admission of guilt as a sinner, the penitent thief was immediately rewarded with the promise of Paradise by Christ Himself. Once he turned to the Savior in total humility and acknowledged the Kingdom of God over which Jesus would reign forever, the thief's faith in the person of Jesus Christ as King was gloriously rewarded with the very words His own disciples would not begin to understand until long after Jesus' resurrection!

One thief chose to follow the world and was shut out of the Kingdom of God, while the other thief turned to Christ and pursued the Kingdom to come. Each man received an immediate consequence upon making his final choice. As the choices for eternity were being waged on the cross between the two thieves, two other men were battling similar choices that would also have eternal consequences. These men were disciples of Jesus Christ who each were confronted with choices to be made under pressures brought on by the darkest hour in history. Peter and John made choices on Calvary that would impact the remainder of their earthly lives in ministry and in the manner of their deaths.

When Christ posed the question to the men in Matthew 16:15 as to His true identity, Peter was the first of the disciples to publicly acknowledge and declare that Jesus was the Son of God. This same man rejected and betrayed Christ, just as Jesus had predicted, when the angry gathering asserted that Peter was one of Christ's followers. Peter had a choice to make, not unlike the thieves who hours later would be hanging next to Christ near death. Tribulation and fear led Peter to make the wrong choice and reject Jesus before a watching world – just as the unrepentant thief joined in with the sneering rulers and mocking soldiers. In that moment, Peter was no different. In that moment, Peter was more concerned about his own life and his own reputation before men than he was about acknowledging the person and the position of Jesus Christ. Ultimately, Peter repented and received the Lord's forgiveness, though his guilt and shame likely remained with him until the very end of his earthly life. According to ecclesiastical history, Peter requested that he be crucified upside down, proclaiming that he was unworthy to die in the same manner as Christ.

The only disciple of Christ to die of natural causes was the disciple who made a vastly different choice at the cross than that of his companions. As his brothers betrayed Christ and fled in fear, the disciple whom Jesus loved (John 13:23) remained near His Lord and Savior, even at the cross. Just hours earlier in the Garden of Gethsemane, the Lord had asked

His beloved disciples to keep watch and pray during His hour of greatest suffering. They fell asleep. In the hours following His arrest, corrupt trials, brutal beatings, and humiliation and condemnation, the men who should have been by Jesus' side to offer support fled in fear and went into hiding. Not one of His disciples walked the hill to Calvary with Him to comfort Him or carry His cross.

What would it have meant to Jesus to see the faces of His brothers in the hostile crowd that morning as He looked down from His cross after being nailed to the tree? Would it not have comforted Christ to see the men whom He had discipled the last three years, kneeling at His feet in prayer to the Father on His behalf? He had just told them the night before at their Passover meal what He must do to accomplish the Father's will. Had they so soon forgotten the words of the Master and betrayed Him just like Judas?

Yet there was one face amidst the sea of mocking soldiers and self-righteous religious rulers that Christ looked upon in those final hours that must have affirmed the Father's love for His Son. The disciple John was not cowering in fear, hidden away in a secret room outside the city walls of Jerusalem. He did not abandon His Lord and seek refuge on a fishing boat upon the Sea of Galilee in order to get away from the angry mobs still seeking to scourge the city of Jesus' followers. John was right there with Jesus at the darkest hour in history, and God had placed Him there to fulfill a divine purpose and plan in the story of redemption and reconciliation.

As Christ looked into the eyes of His beloved disciple John and asked him to care for His mother Mary, He was establishing the model for the family of believers in the body of Christ that would be the church.

> [25]Near the cross of Jesus stood his mother, his mother's sister, Mary the wife of Clopas, and Mary Magdalene. [26]When Jesus saw his mother there, and the disciple whom he loved standing nearby, he said to his mother, "Dear woman, here is your son," [27]and to the disciple, "Here is your mother." From that time on, this disciple took her into his home. (John 19:25-27)

John and Mary were now joined together as family, not by a genetic code of DNA as blood relatives, but by an even stronger tie found only in the sacrificial blood of the Lamb. The Father's will had been accomplished. Different disciples, different choices, vastly different consequences.

Adam and Eve painfully learned that a consequence had to be paid as the price for the choice they made in the Garden. There was an immediate consequence, as well as a far-reaching consequence, for choosing to disobey God and thereby allowing sin to enter the perfect world that the Creator had provided for them in Eden. The most immediate consequence of their pride resulted in the death of an innocent animal to provide the skins for the Lord to cover their nakedness and shame. Another consequence imposed in the moment was banishment from Paradise and from enjoying fellowship with God in the Garden.

The long-term consequences of their choice in believing the lies of Satan were the full effects of sin, suffering, and death on every generation to follow from their offspring that would require blood payment to atone for their choice – a blood payment that would ultimately require the sacrifice of the Father's own Son as a final and full payment to reconcile His children to Himself. Adam and Eve paid a price as a result of their choice for which no pardon could be granted until Christ Himself came into the world to redeem mankind.

The choices we make inevitably have consequences. Some are instantaneous, while others are not recognized as consequences until many years later. In either case, there are consequences to each and every action, each and every choice. Some call it simple cause-and-effect, while others with a theological bent term it the law of reciprocity, referring to the teachings of Christ on reaping the fruit from the seeds that we sow in life. Wrong choices will simply not yield a payback that can equal the blessings from God that flow back to us from the righteous choices we make that are directed by His will from the Holy Spirit. King David experienced the devastating pain of this lesson in his own life after a series of wrong choices.

The greatest king of Israel basked in the blessings of a fruitful reign as king because the Hand of God was upon Him. While King David was known to be a "man after God's own heart," (1 Samuel 13:14) there came a point in his life when he allowed the desires of his own heart to lead him far from the heart of God. In the pursuit of satisfying his own lust and the desires of his flesh, King David pursued the wife of another man, to the lowest point of plotting and arranging her husband's death and then lying about his deeds in order to hide his shame and guilt. One wrong choice, followed by a series of even-more-wrong choices, brought David ultimately to a point of desperate brokenness.

When the prophet Nathan confronted him with his sins, David cried out to God in repentance and admitted that he had sinned against God Himself. David asked for and received the total forgiveness of God, yet he could not escape the consequences of his actions. The price to be paid for David's sins with Bathsheba was the death of their son who was the result of their union.

As in every other instance in the Bible, where there is sin, there is death – "for the wages of sin is death." (Romans 6:23a) The death may occur immediately, as in the case of David and Bathsheba's son, or years later, as in the death of a marriage by divorce when the details of an adulterous affair come to light. While the timing of the consequence may vary, postponing the pain for a season, the consequence itself remains and can not be avoided or eluded. As their earthly lives came to their final breaths, each of the thieves on either side of Christ must surely have experienced this reality upon entering their respective eternal destinations. All choices have unavoidable consequences. Period.

"As I have observed, those who plow evil and those who sow trouble reap it." (Job 4:8)

"Sow for yourselves righteousness, reap the fruit of unfailing love, and break up your unplowed ground; for it is time to seek the LORD, until he comes and showers righteousness on you." (Hosea 10:12)

Lesson #6

We Must First Fear God

But the other answered, and rebuking him said,
"Do you not even fear God...?" (Luke 23:40a)

Upon hearing the mockery and insults spewing forth from the mouth of his fellow criminal, the penitent thief began his rebuke with a single question that pointed directly to the condition of the man's heart: "Do you not even fear God...?" (Luke 23:40) Even hanging near death, the thief bound for paradise could not contain his righteous anger and astonishment that the condemned criminal would speak to Christ in such an irreverent and disrespectful tone. In stating the obvious through his rhetorical question, the penitent thief acknowledged what was clearly missing in the life of his comrade that kept him from having a relationship with God through His Son dying on the cross next to him. Fear of God lies at the foundation of that relationship.

The term "fear of God" refers to that sense of reverence and awe that we experience in His presence, rather than the sort of anxious tension that leads to a "spirit of fear" as described by Paul in 2 Timothy 1:7. This sort of fear, or feeling afraid, leads us away from trusting God toward the destructive path of relying upon self and others for temporary peace and joy. The Bible specifically mentions these two types of fear. The first type of fear stems from a reverence of God's power and glory, as well as a proper respect for His wrath and anger. Fear of the Lord encompasses the very nature of who God is and His divine attributes as we draw closer to Him in relationship and reap lasting peace and joy. The penitent thief embraced this fear of God by trusting Jesus at the end of his earthly life, while the other held fast to his spirit of fear that ultimately led him to eternal destruction.

Fear of the Lord reaps blessings and benefits that are specifically identified in Scripture. This reverential awe of God is the beginning of wisdom and leads to good understanding according to Psalm 111:10 and leads to life, rest, peace, and contentment in Proverbs 19:23. The Book of Wisdom also identifies the fear of God as a refuge for us in 14:26 and as the fountain of life in 14:27. God's Word plainly states the blessings that overflow to those who fear Him:

> So that you, your children and their children after them may fear the Lord your God as long as you live by keeping all his decrees and commands that I give you, and so that you may enjoy long life. (Deut. 6:2)

Let those who fear the Lord say: "His love endures forever." (Psalm 118:4).

Blessed are all who fear the Lord, who walk in his ways. (Psalm 128:1).

"The fear of the Lord adds length to life, but the

years of the wicked are cut short." (Proverbs 10:27).

"He said in a loud voice, 'Fear God and give him glory, because the hour of his judgment has come. Worship him who made the heavens, the earth, the sea and the springs of water.'" (Rev. 14:7).

Isaiah 41:10 encourages us, "Do not fear, for I am with you; Do not anxiously look about you, for I am your God. I will strengthen you, surely I will help you, surely I will uphold you with My righteous right hand." Jesus fulfilled this promise to the penitent thief in his greatest hour of need as he placed his trust in the Savior. In rebuking the hardened heart of the thief who had no fear of God, the thief who repented would ultimately be redeemed, acknowledging his own fear of God as he humbled himself and finally turned to Jesus for help. Yet, the spirit of fear, which led the other thief to mock Jesus, continued to entangle the dying man as he desperately attempted to hold on to his earthly life, forsaking eternity. The spirit of fear can only be overcome by trusting God and embracing His perfect love. "There is no fear in **love**. But **perfect love** drives out fear..." (1 John 4:18) The promise of God in Isaiah 41:10 was surely kept by Jesus in helping, upholding, and delivering the thief to paradise.

One of the most powerful examples from the Old Testament of what it means to trust and fear God completely involves a father and a son whose story of faith and sacrifice would point to the ultimate sacrifice of God's own Son. Abraham and Isaac journeyed to a different hill, at a different point in time, to a different altar, but the intended sacrifice was the same – a beloved son. In total obedience to the Lord's command, Abraham was prepared to sacrifice his long-awaited son as a worship offering to God. The Lord rewarded Abraham's complete faith and trust in God by sparing the boy and sending a substitute sacrifice to take Isaac's place on the altar of sacrifice – just as God would do for us in sending His Son to die on the cross for our sins. Genesis 22:12 records the words spoken by God to Abraham on the altar of sacrifice as he was about to plunge the knife into his son. "Do not lay a hand on the boy," he said. "Do not do anything to him. Now I know that you fear God, because you have not withheld from me your son, your only son." Abraham's fear of the Lord spared the life of his son. The penitent thief's fear of God spared his torment in hell for eternity as Christ rewarded him with eternal life in paradise.

Lesson #7

Sins Must be Acknowledged

*And we indeed are suffering justly, for we are
receiving what we deserve for our deeds.
(Luke 23:41a)*

While one thief sought only to save himself by
challenging Christ to bring them down from
their crosses, the other thief first acknowledged the
fear of God and then proceeded to acknowledge their
guilt as sinners. There would be no need of a Savior if
one were free of sins. What separated the two thieves
on their crosses had not only a physical dimension,
but a spiritual dimension as well. The divine arrange-
ment of the three crosses was God's message to the
world that there is indeed a bridge that connects the
unrighteous with the righteous – Christ is the bridge.
Physically located between the two criminals was
the One who could wipe away their sins and usher
them into Paradise forever.

The spiritual dimension of the thieves' separation centered upon their vastly different perceptions
of themselves as sinners. One refused to be broken
and humbled by his deeds, and proceeded to mockingly demand that Christ save him. He did not turn
to Christ in brokenness and admit his sin and ask for
forgiveness. Rather, he joined the crowd in hurling

insults at the Savior and stubbornly rejected his own guilt by asking that he be spared the consequence he truly deserved.

Before asking to be remembered by Christ, the other thief first acknowledged his guilt as a sinner, proclaiming that he was getting what he deserved as a result of his "deeds." This was a man who had reached a final destination, but who also recognized that God was extending His Hand of redemption to him through Christ. The penitent thief did not offer excuses or attempt to defend his actions prior to asking Jesus to remember him. Rather, he admitted his guilt and acknowledged that he deserved to suffer for the things he had done in his life that had brought him to this moment of hanging on a cross. In the eyes of this thief, justice had been accomplished, and there was no turning back in the hopes of having the consequences removed. He was not seeking an earthly reprieve or pardon that would take him down from the cross to avoid death by suffocation. He had one simple request: to be remembered. After first publicly acknowledging his guilt as a sinner, he simply turned to Jesus and asked to be remembered by Christ when He assumed His rightful place as the Ruler of His Kingdom.

We must do the same. Before we can expect God to forget our offenses and bestow the riches and splendor of heaven upon us for all eternity, there is one important admission we must make to God and to those whom we have offended: that we are sinners. Two of the most difficult phrases for humans to vocalize are "I was wrong" and "I am sorry." Far greater energy, and far more words, are expended on justifying and defending our wrong actions in order to avoid admitting that we are simply wrong. Pride fuels the sin nature through attempts by the person to save face in the eyes of others, as if a confession of wrongdoing somehow makes the person look weak.

As examined earlier, King David only experienced reconciliation with God after he acknowledged his sins of adultery, murder, and lying. David reached the point of brokenness where he no longer attempted fabrication of excuses to justify his sinful behaviors. Because of his relationship with God, David once again pursued the Heart of God with all of his own heart, mind, and body by acknowledging that his sins had been committed directly against God. In despair and total repentance, David cried out to his Father for forgiveness. Psalm 51 pours out the broken heart of David after he was confronted by the prophet Nathan over his sins, and poignantly paints the repentant heart and broken spirit with which we must approach God after we have sinned and are seeking His forgiveness.

> [1] Have mercy on me, O God,
>> according to your unfailing love;
>> according to your great compassion
>> blot out my transgressions.
>
> [2] Wash away all my iniquity
>> and cleanse me from my sin.
>
> [3] For I know my transgressions,
>> and my sin is always before me.

4 Against you, you only, have I sinned
   and done what is evil in your sight,
   so that you are proved right when you speak
   and justified when you judge.

5 Surely I was sinful at birth,
   sinful from the time my mother conceived me.

6 Surely you desire truth in the inner parts;
   you teach me wisdom in the inmost place.

7 Cleanse me with hyssop, and I will be clean;
   wash me, and I will be whiter than snow.

8 Let me hear joy and gladness;
   let the bones you have crushed rejoice.

9 Hide your face from my sins
   and blot out all my iniquity.

10 Create in me a pure heart, O God,
    and renew a steadfast spirit within me.

11 Do not cast me from your presence
    or take your Holy Spirit from me.

12 Restore to me the joy of your salvation
    and grant me a willing spirit, to sustain me.

13 Then I will teach transgressors your ways,
    and sinners will turn back to you.

14 Save me from bloodguilt, O God,
    the God who saves me,
    and my tongue will sing of your righteousness.

15 O Lord, open my lips,
    and my mouth will declare your praise.

16 You do not delight in sacrifice, or I would bring
    it;

you do not take pleasure in burnt offerings.

¹⁷ The sacrifices of God are a broken spirit;
a broken and contrite heart,
O God, you will not despise.

¹⁸ In your good pleasure make Zion prosper;
build up the walls of Jerusalem.

¹⁹ Then there will be righteous sacrifices,
whole burnt offerings to delight you;
then bulls will be offered on your altar.

In order for the healing process of forgiveness to begin in the life of the sinner, the sins must first be acknowledged and confessed. How can a sick patient seek healing if they refuse to acknowledge that they have an illness? The same may be said of sin in our lives. The Father will not blot out our transgressions if we fail to acknowledge them. Those who rationalize and justify their actions, pretending that they are sinless, will continue living out their lives saddled with the sickness of sin. God's gift of complete forgiveness begins with the simple act of confession.

Therefore confess your sins to each other and pray for each other so that you may be healed. The prayer of a righteous man is powerful and effective. (James 5:6)

Many also of those who had believed kept coming, confessing and disclosing their practices."(Acts 19:18)

We know that God does not hear sinners;

but if anyone is God-fearing and does His will, He hears him. (John 9:31)

And all the country of Judea was going out to him, and all the people of Jerusalem; and they were being baptized by him in the Jordan River, confessing their sins. (Mark 1:5)

Lesson #8

Words Must Be Spoken

And he was saying, "Jesus, remember me when You come in Your kingdom!" (Luke 23:42)

In his moment of greatest need, the penitent thief did not simply hang his head in submission and quietly meditate upon how he had hoped things might have been different in his life. The time for quiet contemplation and reflection had long passed as he found himself nailed to a tree faced with agonizing physical death. It was a time for action, despite the present circumstances of being rendered immobile by his own crucifixion.

Most assuredly, this was a man who had many times either run from desperate situations to escape capture or who had talked his way out of a predicament in order to gain a reprieve. His words were all he had left to make one last attempt at rectifying a life of wrong choices that had led him to Calvary that morning to face death on a cross next to two other condemned men. The glorious difference this time was that one of the men was the Son of God who was preparing to come into His Kingdom. This time, the words he would speak in his remaining breaths on earth would affect his next life in eternity. This time, the words would fall upon the ears of the only One who could truly grant the one pardon that would last forever. The power of words could only have been more fully understood by the One who was the Word made flesh.

> ¹In the beginning was the Word, and the Word was with God, and the Word was God. ²He was with God in the beginning. ³Through him all things were made; without him nothing was made that has been made. ⁴In him was life, and that life was the light of men. ⁵The light shines in the darkness, but the darkness has not understood it…

> ¹⁴The Word became flesh and made his dwelling among us. We have seen his glory, the glory of the One and Only, who came from the Father, full of grace and truth. (John 1:1-5, 14)

Following the thief's rebuke of his partner and confession of his own sin, he addressed Christ directly with the words that would ultimately bestow upon himself the greatest gift of all. "Jesus, remember me when You come in Your kingdom!" (Luke 23:42) Those nine words contained both a petition and a proclamation, phrased in a particular manner as only God could orchestrate. The penitent thief used those final breaths to address Jesus by name, make a final request, and ultimately acknowledge the person and position of Christ as King – a King who would be coming into His Kingdom AFTER His death. This common thief understood the mission and ministry of Christ in a way that His own disciples never fully grasped until after Jesus' ascension into Heaven from the Mt. of Olives.

This man knew, without any doubt or hesitation, that Jesus Christ was a King. With only moments remaining in his earthly life, he had no time for doubt or hesitation. This was the precise moment that God had prepared for him before forming him in his mother's womb. And this moment required words – not random thoughts, good intentions toward future actions, nor subtle gestures and body language. The thief formed and vocalized the words from his mouth that had come directly from his heart, and he addressed them directly to the Savior of the World, as a subject would address his King.

The petition to the King consisted of two words: "remember me." He did not ask to be rescued from his earthly position on the cross in order to resume his worldly existence. He did not ask for power, riches, or second chances. He simply looked out into a future and asked to be remembered. A future? Surely, if there were one man without any hope or prospects of a future, it would be the one bound to a tree, bleeding and breathless, facing certain death. Yet, this man indeed had every hope of a future, because he acknowledged in his final moments that his eternal life was in the Hands of the One hanging beside him, who would be coming into His Kingdom after this present life.

Those within earshot of this dying man's final request would have certainly thought it bizarre that he would be asking a soon-to-be-dead, fellow criminal something one would only ask from the living – to be remembered. How does a dead man *remember*? He doesn't. Only the *living* have the capacity to remember. The thief's eyes were opened to something about which most in the crowd that day remained in darkness. Those closest to Jesus, who had abandoned Him and were literally in hiding, also remained in darkness over the defining event of Jesus' earthly ministry. Jesus the King would not remain in death. He would overcome sin and death and come back to life in order to be seated in glory in His Kingdom to Come. The Resurrection would allow Jesus to remember the thief who had spoken those powerful words next to Him that day, and then one day gather him and all other believers to Paradise for all eternity.

Had the thief not first recognized his need of a Savior, those two words would never have fallen from his lips in those last moments. His request to Jesus came only after he had confessed his guilt as a sinner for the deeds he had committed that had earned him a place on the cross. The two-word petition to be remembered also came after his declaration that Jesus was innocent. In the same breath of acknowledging his guilt and just punishment, the thief on the cross declared that Jesus had done nothing wrong. The spotless Lamb was being sacrificed for him, and for all other sinners. "All have sinned and fall short of the glory of God." (Romans 3:23)

The collection of verses in Paul's letter to the Romans that outline the path to salvation is often referred to as the "Romans Road to Salvation." These four verses appropriately draw comparisons to the manner in which ancient Roman roads were constructed, in four distinct layers of sand, gravel, stones, and paving blocks. Many of these ancient roads remain traveled today, centuries after they were constructed. These same roads allowed the Gospel to travel to unreached peoples with the life-saving message of hope in fulfillment of the Great Commission to spread the news of Jesus Christ.

The four verses are Romans 3:23, 6:23, 5:8, and 10:9. These life-giving words breathed by God to Paul lead the lost down the road to eternal life. While the thief on the cross may have traveled the darkest Roman road imaginable in the form of crucifixion, the cruelest of Roman punishments handed down to condemned men, he traveled another "Roman Road" that day which led to streets paved with gold – in Paradise. By acknowledging his own sinful state while also declaring his fear of God, the thief recognized the basic truth that Paul would write about 30 years later, that "all have sinned and fall short of the Glory of God." (Romans 3:23) By accepting his "sentence of condemnation" in publicly recognizing that he was receiving what he deserved for his deeds, the thief testified to the law of God established in the Garden of Eden that "the wages of sin is death." (Romans 6:23)

He was paying that price on the cross next to Jesus, who was also dying under that same sentence of condemnation despite His innocence, as proclaimed by the one for whom Christ was laying down His life.

Paul wrote of this divine circumstance in Romans 5:8 – "But God demonstrates his own love for us in this: While we were still sinners, Christ died for us." And in the final words spoken by the thief on the cross, he traveled upon that final layer of the Roman Road that would transport him to Paradise after his physical death. By confessing with his mouth and believing in his heart that Jesus had the power to remember him when Christ came into His Kingdom, the penitent thief was saved and received the glorious gift of eternal life that Paul would describe in Romans 10:9 – "That if you confess with your mouth, 'Jesus is Lord,' and believe in your heart that God raised him from the dead, you will be saved." Though he had traveled many wrong roads in his earthly existence, the final road upon which the thief traveled was the only road paved with the blood of Jesus Christ that could deliver him from his sinful state and carry him to Paradise, washed clean and as white as snow by the blood of the Lamb.

"Though your sins are like scarlet, they shall be as white as snow; though they are red as crimson, they shall be like wool." (Isaiah 1:18)

God's promise to all of us in Romans 10:13 states that "everyone who calls upon the name of the Lord will be saved." Can it possibly be that simple? Yes. Simple for us, though it was Christ who paid the penalty and endured the suffering and shame in order to make it that simple for us. To call upon Jesus means simply to ask Him in prayer. The verse requires nothing else of us other than exactly what the thief did on Calvary: call upon Jesus and ask Him.

Lesson #9

Jesus Will Answer

And He said to him, "Truly I say to you, today you shall be with Me in Paradise." (Luke 23:43)

Jesus did not remain silent on the cross when He was addressed by the penitent thief with his petition to be remembered. The same love and compassion that led Christ to respond to those demonstrating genuine faith in Him when asking for a miracle is the same compassion that led Jesus to answer the thief, even in His state of suffering on the edge of physical death. Christ did not ignore the request of this new believer and follower. He did not turn away from him and focus upon the blind souls hurling insults at his feet. They were lost, but next to Him was one sheep that was found. Jesus answered him, and the lost sheep listened to the life-saving words that he had hoped would come from the Savior's lips. "…Truly I say to you, today you shall be with Me in Paradise." (Luke 23:43)

Just hours earlier, Christ had remained silent when standing before His accusers in the series of corrupt trials that led to His death sentence for treason and blasphemy. Jesus did not defend Himself before the Sanhedrin, Pontius Pilate, or Herod, even when given the opportunity to display His divine nature and prove that He was indeed the Messiah. As in the words of the prophet Isaiah, He stood there silent, "led like a lamb to the slaughter, and as a sheep before her shearers is silent."

> He was oppressed and afflicted,
> yet he did not open his mouth;
> he was led like a lamb to the slaughter,
> and as a sheep before her shearers is
> silent, so he did not open his mouth.
> (Isaiah 53:7)

> The watchman opens the gate for him,
> and the sheep listen to his voice. He
> calls his own sheep by name and leads
> them out. When he has brought out all
> his own, he goes on ahead of them, and
> his sheep follow him because they know
> his voice. (John 10:3-4)

> But when he, the Spirit of truth, comes,
> he will guide you into all truth. He will
> not speak on his own; he will speak only
> what he hears, and he will tell you what
> is yet to come." (John 16:13)

> But the Counselor, the Holy Spirit,
> whom the Father will send in my name,
> will teach you all things and will remind
> you of everything I have said to you.
> (John 14:26)

It is written: "I believed; therefore I have spoken." With that same spirit of faith we also believe and therefore speak.... (2 Corinthians 4:13)

Lesson #10

The Eternal Result is Immediate

Jesus did not respond to the penitent thief's request to be remembered by saying "I'll get back with you on that." Christ did not reply with a list of conditions that must be first met before the promise of Paradise was granted. The response was not a lengthy list of works to be accomplished with a minimum passing score to somehow earn an admissions ticket through the gates of Heaven. No, Christ immediately responded with a guarantee by His Word that the thief would be with Him in Paradise.

The faith in Christ demonstrated by the thief in asking Jesus to remember him is what saved the thief from spending eternity in torment, separated from God. He would not have the opportunity to come down from the cross and suddenly live a new life filled with good works and acts of kindness to his fellow man. The thief was engaged in only one final act before leaving the earth – the act of dying. Good deeds or gaining favor with the Pharisees would not earn salvation for the thief. Only his faith in the One dying next to him would bring him to Paradise.

[8]For it is by grace you have been saved, through faith—and this not from your-

selves, it is the gift of God— [9]not by works, so that no one can boast. (Ephesians 2:8-9)

[13]And you, who were dead in trespasses and the uncircumcision of your flesh, God made alive together with him, having forgiven us all our trespasses, [14] having canceled the bond which stood against us with its legal demands; this he set aside, nailing it to the cross. [15]He disarmed the principalities and powers and made a public example of them, triumphing over them in him. (Col. 2:13-15)

Lesson #11

Jesus is King and Kinsman Redeemer

The penitent thief believed by faith that Jesus was truly a king. His request to be remembered by Jesus upon coming into His Kingdom naturally assumes that he believed he was directing his petition to none other than a king. Was it the inscription hanging over His head – one last mockery by Pilate toward the Pharisees? Had the thief encountered Christ and His ministry on a previous occasion? Did God reveal to the thief that this man dying on the cross next to him was indeed the Son of God, King of Kings and Lord of Lords?

The penitent thief used his final breaths on the cross of shame not only to address Jesus by name and make a final request to be remembered, but also to ultimately acknowledge the person and position of Christ as King – a King who would be coming into His Kingdom AFTER His death. This common thief understood the mission and ministry of Christ in a way that His own disciples never fully grasped until after Jesus' ascension into Heaven from the Mt. of Olives. This King would defeat sin and death through His miraculous resurrection three days after being taken down from the cross of shame and placed in a borrowed tomb. By doing so, Jesus fulfilled His promise to the thief – and to all who call upon the name of Jesus by faith to save them from their sins – that he would redeem him and spend eternity with him in Paradise. Jesus was his "Kinsman Redeemer."

The practice of a close relative paying the debt of a family member in order to redeem him from a life of servitude was a legal concept appearing in the Old Testament under the Law of Moses. Meaning to redeem or buy back, the Hebrew word *Goel* translates as "nearest kinsman" or "kinsman redeemer."[13] Provision was made in the Law of Moses for the poor person who was forced to sell part of his property or himself into slavery. His nearest of kin could "buy back" what his relative was forced to sell (Leviticus 25:48). Usually a wealthy benefactor, the kinsman redeemer freed the debtor by paying what could be termed the "ransom price." "If a fellow countryman of yours becomes so poor he has to sell part of his property, then his nearest kinsman is to come and buy back what his relative has sold."

One of the most beautiful passages where the word *Goel* is found is in the life of Naomi in the book of Ruth, which poignantly tells the story of Naomi's *Goel*, Boaz. Naomi was the poorest person in Israel, but her kinsman was the richest. She and her daughters-in-law lost their homestead and income after the death of her husband and two sons. Deeply sensing the loss of her homeland and

---

13   goel. Dictionary.com. Easton's 1897 Bible Dictionary. http://dictionary.reference.com/browse/goel (accessed: Feb. 8, 2012).

relatives, Naomi was living in a foreign land and became bitter. The closest kinsman to the family had the first right to Naomi's property, and the next in line was Boaz. Should Ruth's closer relative choose not to redeem or purchase the property, Boaz was prepared to do so. The rightful kinsman redeemer agreed to redeem the piece of land until he learned there was a young widow involved in the transaction, causing him to ultimately back out of serving in the role of redeemer. Boaz remained as the legal nearest of kin who had the privilege of redeeming both her land and the widow herself. The Moabitess and the Jew became one. Because Boaz was nearest of kin to her deceased husband (Ruth 2:1), he was both willing and financially able to serve as *Goel* by paying the price of redemption (2:1 and 4:4).

Under Mosaic Law, four requirements were specified for a kinsman to redeem:

- He must be closest of kin (Leviticus 25:48; 25:25 Ruth 3:12–13).

- He must be of financial means to be able to redeem (Ruth 4:4–6), in addition to not being in need of redemption himself.

- He must demonstrate a clear willingness to redeem (Ruth 4:6).

- Redemption was completed when the price was paid in full (Leviticus 25:27; Ruth 4:7-11).

Jesus Christ served as the *Goel*, the Kinsman Redeemer, for all mankind. He met all four requirements of Mosaic Law and paid the price in full with His own blood as the ransom for reconciling us to the Father. By robing Himself in human flesh and identifying Himself with sinners even though He was sinless, Jesus came into the world as our nearest kinsman through the incarnation so that our sin debt with God could be paid in full. "For what the Law could not do, weak as it was through the flesh, God *did*: sending His own Son in the likeness of sinful flesh and *as an offering* for sin, He condemned sin in the flesh." (Romans 8:3) Jesus left the splendor of Heaven to identify with sinful men and "emptied Himself, taking the form of a bond-servant, *and* being made in the likeness of men." (Philippians 2:7)

The second requirement was met in that only Christ could serve as the spotless Lamb to be sacrificed and offered up to God in reconciliation of mankind as the ransom to be paid for the sin that entered the world through Adam and Eve. The Old Testament cycle of sacrifices and sin offerings ended with the blood of Christ spilled out on Calvary when He took our place on the cross as the atoning sacrifice for our sins. God formed a new covenant with man through the blood of His Son. "For you know the grace of our Lord Jesus Christ, that though He was rich, yet for your sake He became poor, so that you through His poverty might become rich." (2 Corinthians 8:9)

Jesus **willingly** went to the cross in complete and total obedience to the will of the Father. He agonized over what He had to do in the Garden of Gethsemane when He asked His Father if there were another way to accomplish the atonement. By asking God to take the cup from Him, He sought the Father's Heart on finding the way to avoid the separation from God that He was about to experience in becoming the sin of the world. Nevertheless, He prayed that the Father's will be done, not His own, as He voluntarily labored up the hill carrying the cross of shame and suffering to serve as our substitute sacrifice.

> For this reason the Father loves Me, because I lay down My life so that I may take it again. No one has taken it away from Me, but I lay it down on My own initiative. I have authority to lay it down, and I have authority to take it up again. This commandment I received from My Father. (John 10:17-18)

Finally, the blood of Jesus Christ satisfied the full price that was to be paid to reconcile the thief on the cross, and all of us, back to the Father and restore the relationship that was broken in Eden. The price was paid in full and never to be paid again. "For God so loved the world that He gave His only begotten Son, that whoever believes in Him shall not perish, but have eternal life." (John 3:16) The invitation remains open today as Jesus continues to offer Himself as the sinner's nearest kinsman. Something also remains to be done on the part of the sinner: traveling down the Romans Road. There is still a responsibility for the sinner to surrender at the feet of our *Goel,* and say, "Cover me with your blood and grace." (Ruth 3:9) Just as the thief asked to be remembered by Jesus, the sinner must ask Jesus into his heart and his life in order to be in Paradise.

In Him we have redemption through His blood, the forgiveness of our trespasses, according to the riches of His grace which He lavished on us. (Ephesians 1:7)

As Naomi held her grandson in her arms, her neighbors exclaimed, "A son has been born to Naomi!" The boy was named Obed, the father of Jesse, the father of King David (Ruth 4:17), of the lineage of the Messiah, Jesus Christ (Matthew 1:5). God had redeemed her by providing a kinsman redeemer in the person of Boaz. The words of Naomi's friends are a reminder of God's grace in our lives when He instituted the new covenant in the blood of Christ. "Blessed is the LORD who has not left you without a redeemer today, and may his name become famous in Israel." (Ruth 4:14) His Name is indeed like no other, and that name means that our salvation comes from the Lord. "Salvation is found in no one else, for there is no other name under heaven given to men by which we must be saved." (Acts 4:12) There is no one like Jesus. The thief on the cross had the privilege of dying in the company of the only One who could give him a new life through His blood. The thief's new life began that day on Calvary when Jesus conquered sin and death once and for all.

Lesson #12

"Come Just As You Are"

As the song of invitation says, "Come just as you are." Do not wait until you have your proverbial act together, for it will never happen that way. The penitent thief obviously had no other choice in approaching the Savior exactly the way he was. He could not clean himself up or change his present circumstance of being nailed to a tree in order to somehow "make a good impression" on the King. The time had long passed for him to concern himself with such superficial, worldly concerns. His remaining moments were few and this would be his last opportunity to come to Christ with his request to be remembered by Jesus when He came into His Kingdom.

Had the thief thought for a moment that his life would have ended hanging on a tree, he would have run to Jesus much earlier with the same request when he had a life left to live. How vastly different that life would have been had he come to Jesus before taking the road that sentenced him to death. The thief may well have avoided the roads that led him to Calvary, but God had a specific purpose and plan for the thief's life to encounter Christ exactly in the way that he did. God chose to paint the most vivid illustration possible of what it truly means to come to Jesus exactly as we are in our present state.

> *Come just as you are*
> *Hear the spirit call*
> *Come just as you are*
> *Come and see*
> *Come recieve*
> *come and live forever*
>
> *Life everlasting*
> *Strength for today*
> *Taste the living water*
> *And never thirst again*
> *Come and see*
> *Come recieve*
> *Come and live forever*

—Come Just As You Are, Joseph Sabolick

A decision to come to Jesus and make Him your King should never be postponed in the hopes that you will be able to "fix" yourself prior to coming to Him. If we were able to accomplish this cleansing on our own, we would have no need for the Savior to extend His grace to us in doing what He accomplished at Calvary and then rising from the dead three days later. Why not come to Him as we are and allow Him to "fix" our brokenness? Could there possibly be anyone more qualified than the Creator Himself? Don't delay and put off a decision for Christ, thinking that worldly wisdom and wealth will satisfy your soul. You'll miss out on the only joy in this lifetime that can truly satisfy – the joy of living for Jesus in the present and of being in His presence for eternity in Paradise, just as a thief learned 2000 years ago on a cross next to the very Source of our joy.

Just as I Am, Without One Plea
By: Charlotte Elliott

Just as I am, without one plea
But that thy blood was shed for me
And that thou bidd'st me come to thee
O Lamb of God, I come, I come.

Just as I am and waiting not
To rid my soul of one dark blot,
To thee, whose blood can cleanse each spot,
O Lamb of God, I come, I come.

Just as I am, though tossed about
With many a conflict, many a doubt,
Fightings and fears within, without,
O Lamb of God, I come, I come.

Just as I am, poor, wretched, blind;
Sight, riches, healing of the mind,
Yea, all I need, in thee to find,
O Lamb of God, I come, I come.

Just as I am, thou wilt receive,
Wilt welcome, pardon, cleanse, relieve;
Because thy promise I believe,
O Lamb of God, I come, I come.

Just a I am; thy love unknown
Has broken every barrier down;
Now to be thine, yea, thine alone,
O Lamb of God, I come, I come.

VI

Hermeneutics: Living out the Lessons in Daily Life – Weaving the Lessons Together

Having previously undertaken the exegesis of the thief passage in Luke, we now turn to the hermeneutics, as we seek to apply the meaning of the verses to our daily lives in the here-and-now. We have explored the twelve life-lessons that emerge from a closer look at the five verses recounting the exchange between Christ and the thieves in Luke 23. How do we now take those lessons learned and practically apply them within the tapestry of our daily lives in such a way that our faith is transformed into the fabric of Hebrews 11:1 – "Now faith is being sure of what we hope for and certain of what we do not see."

Clearly, the penitent thief was certain of the kingdom that he could not physically see on the day that he approached the King and asked to be remembered. Faith led him to make that final request. Certainly, the thief was sure that the One to whom he made the request had the power to grant him a place in that kingdom. Faith confirmed for him that his hopes would become reality upon taking that final breath. The application of the twelve lessons begins with stepping forward in faith. Ultimately, faith is the common thread that ties the twelve lessons together within that tapestry of our daily lives.

As we have examined, the lessons illustrated in the exchange between Christ and the thief portray the humble attitude and broken human spirit with which we are all to approach the Savior in asking for His forgiveness and remembrance. This life-saving exchange of words between two men nailed to trees was nothing short of an act of worship by the penitent thief. Such an act of worship was the direct expression of the mustard seed of faith planted in the heart of the penitent thief by the One to whom the worship was directed. Those final moments in the life of the thief were devoted to the worship of the King – moments that would prepare him for an eternity of glorious worship of the Lamb in Paradise.

The twelve lessons revealed at the site of the three crosses engage all four dimensions than uniquely define mankind, made in the very image of the Creator. Applying the lessons in our daily lives involves the four aspects of a human being's makeup that are identified in Luke 2:52. Just as "Jesus grew in wisdom and stature, and in favor with God and men," we must continually develop intellectually, physically, spiritually, and socially if we are to fully realize the potential that God has coded within our DNA when He formed us in the womb. Heart, mind, body, and soul were fully engaged in the conversion of the penitent thief on Calvary.

Taken together, the twelve lessons reflect a divine process that takes a person from the valley to the mountaintop by first engaging the heart and mind through faith. When a person arrives at that point of brokenness over his sin, the lessons taught by the penitent thief's words and actions on the cross take on practical meaning and application. First, intellectual reasoning confirms the realization that a choice for or against Christ must ultimately be made – there is no avoiding the choice. While even one breath remains in a person's life, it truly is not too late to make the choice. This reality serves to lift one of the greatest burdens and hindrances keeping people from coming to Jesus. Once the mind has grasped the fact that God does not keep a record of wrongs for those who come to Him for forgiveness, the realization takes hold of their hearts that allows them to surrender their past lives and eventually their wills to God. Nothing they have done in their pasts can keep them from the Savior. He supplies the faith required for this surrender, and in exchange He grants us His peace.

For the mind to then allow the body to respond to the Savior's calling, the person's heart must first have been cultivated with seeds of faith that point toward that reverence and awe for God we call fear. The planting of those seeds offers yet another lesson to those who have already made the choice to follow Christ – investing in the lives of those who appear to be lost without hope. Salvation comes after the heart has been prepared to receive and accept the message of the Good News. This message often comes from the foot soldiers of Christ who carry the message of redemption to those who are lost in the world. The seeds that are planted may not be harvested until years later when the person is ready to surrender his life to Jesus, but the fact remains that the seeds must be sown in obedience to the Great Commission given by Jesus to His disciples after His resurrection from the dead.

> The kingdom of heaven is like a mustard seed, which a man took and planted in his field. [32]Though it is the smallest of all your seeds, yet when it grows, it is the largest of garden plants and becomes a tree, so that the birds of the air come and perch in its branches. (Matthew 13:31, 32)

> Therefore go and make disciples of all nations, baptizing them in the name of the Father and of the Son and of the Holy Spirit, [20]and teaching them to obey everything I have commanded you. And surely I am with you always, to the very end of the age. (Matthew 28: 19, 20)

Once the heart and mind have purposed to respond, the body then acts upon the leading of the Holy Spirit to travel down the Romans Road traversed by the thief on the cross. Having acknowledged in heart and mind that every choice and every action has a consequence, the person coming to Christ, now ready to make that decision, must believe, confess, and ask: 1) Believe and proclaim that Christ died for sin and rose from the dead; 2) Confess that he is a sinner in need of a Savior; and 3) Ask Jesus to forgive him and become part of His forever family. Having acknowledged the sin and spoken the words, Jesus responds and salvation is accomplished. Access to the throne of heaven through the blood of Christ is immediately granted to the newest member of Paradise, just as it was given to the thief who simply asked to be remembered by the King, the Kinsman Redeemer.

The passage to Paradise begins with one simple act: coming forward. We cannot expect to be remembered by Jesus if we do not take that first step and come to Jesus – just as we are. While the world will tell us there are many roads that lead to heaven, the truth of God's Word plainly states that there is but one way to the Father in Heaven. Many mistakenly believe that they are part of some benevolent god's family, when in fact they are simply believing the same lies from the serpent that led Adam and Eve into sin and death. "I am the way and the truth and the life. No one comes to the Father except through Me." (John 14:6) Coming to Jesus is the only way. In following the example of the thief, we must come to Christ, humbled and broken, as though we too were surrendering our last breaths as the penalty for our crimes. Were we to take on such an attitude of finality, we would race to Jesus and beg to be remembered. Hearing those words that He uttered to the thief that day would be the sweet music of heaven. The alternative is to be eternally forsaken, when instead the words fall forth from Jesus' lips to those who chose not to come to Him, that He never knew them. Which words do you want to hear?

[22]Many will say to me on that day, 'Lord, Lord, did we not prophesy in your name, and in your name drive out demons and perform many miracles?' [23]Then I will tell them plainly, 'I never knew you. Away from me, you evildoers!' (Matthew 7:22-23)

[40]The King will reply, "I tell you the truth, whatever you did for one of the least of these brothers of mine, you did for me. [41]Then he will say to those on his left, "Depart from me, you who are cursed, into the eternal fire prepared for the devil and his angels." (Matthew 25:40-41)

VII

The Romans Road and a Sinner's Prayer

The collection of verses in Paul's letter to the Romans that outline the path to salvation is often referred to as the "Romans Road to Salvation." These four verses appropriately draw comparisons to the manner in which ancient Roman roads were constructed, in four distinct layers of sand, gravel, stones, and paving blocks. Many of these ancient roads remain traveled today, centuries after they were constructed. These same roads allowed the Gospel to travel to unreached peoples with the life-saving message of hope in fulfillment of the Great Commission to spread the news of Jesus Christ.

The four verses are Romans 3:23, 6:23, 5:8, and 10:9. These life-giving words breathed by God to Paul lead the lost down the road to eternal life. While the thief on the cross may have traveled the darkest Roman road imaginable in the form of crucifixion, the cruelest of Roman punishments handed down to condemned men, he traveled another "Roman Road" that day which led to streets paved with gold – in Paradise. By acknowledging his own sinful state while also declaring his fear of God, the thief recognized the basic truth that Paul would write about

30 years later, that "all have sinned and fall short of the Glory of God." (Romans 3:23) By accepting his "sentence of condemnation" in publicly recognizing that he was receiving what he deserved for his deeds, the thief testified to the law of God established in the Garden of Eden that "the wages of sin is death." (Romans 6:23)

He was paying that price on the cross next to Jesus, who was also dying under that same sentence of condemnation despite His innocence, as proclaimed by the one for whom Christ was laying down His life. Paul wrote of this divine circumstance in Romans 5:8 – "But God demonstrates his own love for us in this: While we were still sinners, Christ died for us." And in the final words spoken by the thief on the cross, he traveled upon that final layer of the Roman Road that would transport him to Paradise after his physical death. By confessing with his mouth and believing in his heart that Jesus had the power to remember him when Christ came into His Kingdom, the penitent thief was saved and received the glorious gift of eternal life that Paul would describe in Romans 10:9 – "That if you confess with your mouth, 'Jesus is Lord,' and believe in your heart that God raised him from the dead, you will be saved." Though he had traveled many wrong roads in his earthly existence, the final road upon which the thief traveled was the only road paved with the blood of Jesus Christ that could deliver him from his sinful state and carry him to Paradise, washed clean and as white as snow by the blood of the Lamb.

Calling on the Name of Jesus: The Sinner's Prayer

The person who has arrived at the point of the thief, in standing ready to place his complete faith and trust in Jesus, is able to then confess that faith with his mouth and respond affirmatively, without hesitation, to the following questions:

Do you acknowledge that your are a sinner?
I am a sinner.
Do you believe by faith that Jesus, God's Son, died for your sin on the cross?
Jesus died for my sin on the cross.
Will you now confess Him as your Savior and Lord?
I accept and proclaim Him as my Lord and my Savior!

God's promise to all of us in Romans 10:13 states that "everyone who calls upon the name of the Lord will be saved." Can it possibly be that simple? Yes. Simple for us, though it was Christ who paid the penalty and endured the suffering and shame in order to make it that simple for us. To call upon Jesus means simply to ask Him in prayer. The verse requires nothing else of us other than exactly what the thief did on Calvary: call upon Jesus and ask Him.

If you are not able to point to a time in your life when you called upon Jesus and prayed to Him, **will you call upon Jesus now to save you from your sin so that you can know God's love and forgiveness forever?**

Call upon the name of Jesus and pray like this: *"Dear God, I confess that I am a sinner. I am sorry and I need a Savior because I know that I cannot save myself. I believe by faith that Jesus, your Son, died on the cross to be my Savior. I believe He rose from the dead on the third day and now lives with you in Heaven awaiting His return to bring us Home. From this moment forward, I turn from my sin and I ask You, Lord Jesus, to forgive my sin and come and live inside my heart. I trust you as my Savior and receive you into my life as my Lord. Thank you, Jesus, for saving me."*

When anyone calls on the Lord in this way, **that person is saved according to God's Word**. If you just prayed this prayer of repentance and faith, or spoke something similar to God, **you are saved**. You have God's everlasting promise on your salvation as recorded in His Word. If you have prayed this prayer to receive Christ as your Lord and Savior, I encourage you to share this life-changing news right now with family and friends. I also encourage you to write down the date you prayed this prayer, so that you will never forget the day you were spiritually born and became part of God's forever family. The day will come when Satan seeks to attack you and cause you to doubt that you were ever saved. You will have a written record to affirm and encourage you in your salvation decision that will strengthen your faith. This will also serve to once again defeat the enemy by certifying that he is indeed a liar. One of the best places to record the date you made the decision to trust Christ and prayed to receive Him is on the inside cover of your Bible. If you do not own one, get a good translation of the living Word of God and begin reading this "love letter" from God. You now have the Holy Spirit living inside you, just as Jesus promised, and He will guide you through His Word and bring meaning to each verse. As in any new relationship, the way you will come to know God is by spending time with Him in prayer and in His Word. This is the way you will come to know His heart. Write the following prayer in your Bible, inserting your name and the date you became part of His family.

> *Believing by faith that God loves me and sent His Son, Jesus Christ, to die for my sin and rise from the tomb to live in me, I, _____, on this date, _____, repent of my sin and accept Jesus Christ as my personal Lord and Savior. According to God's promise in Romans 10:13, I have called upon His name and have His word for the assurance of my salvation.*

The glorious news is twofold: you are now guaranteed a place in Paradise forever, where you will worship Jesus forever and be in His presence. Secondly, nothing can separate you from this promise or cause you to lose your place in Heaven. God's promise includes His word that there is absolutely nothing in heaven or earth that can separate you from this eternal love in Jesus Christ. This promise that is sealed in the new covenant of Christ's blood was recorded for us again by Paul in his letter to the Romans.

> [31]What, then, shall we say in response to this? If God is for us, who can be against us? [32]He who did not spare his own Son, but gave him up for us all—how will he not also, along with him, graciously give us all things? [33]Who will bring any charge against those whom God has chosen? It is God who justifies. [34]Who is he that condemns? Christ Jesus, who died— more than that, who was raised to life— is at the right hand of God and is also interceding for us. [35]Who shall separate us from the love of Christ? Shall trouble or hardship or persecution or famine or nakedness or danger or sword? [36]As it is written: "For your sake we face death all day long; we are considered as sheep to be slaughtered." [37]No, in all these things we are more than conquerors through him who loved us. [38]For I am convinced that neither death nor life, neither angels nor demons, neither the present nor the future, nor any powers, [39]neither height nor depth, nor anything else in all creation, will be able to separate us from the love of God that is in Christ Jesus our Lord." (Romans 8:31-39)

About the Author

With 15 years teaching experience and 15 years of corporate experience, educator, author, and violinist Jeff Valerioti has been blessed in the last ten of these years to shepherd students in the classroom as a Bible teacher. He earned a Master's Degree in Theological Studies at Liberty University and is a licensed and ordained minister of the Gospel. Prior to entering ministry, Jeff served as Director of Internet for Reader's Digest and VP of Interactive Marketing for a subsidiary of Ameritrade. Jeff also teaches a graduate writing course for Liberty University, in addition to playing and teaching violin in the metro Atlanta area, where he resides with his wife and two children.

www.ingramcontent.com/pod-product-compliance
Lightning Source LLC
Chambersburg PA
CBHW062008040426
42447CB00010B/1974